Dog's Life Colouring Book
First published in Great Britain in 2017 by
Graffeg Limited, 24 Stradey Park Business
Centre, Mwrwg Road, Llangennech, Llanelli,
Carmarthenshire SA14 8YP Wales UK.
Tel +44 (0)1554 824000 www.graffeg.com
Illustrated by Helen Elliott © copyright 2016
Designed and produced by Graffeg Limited
© copyright 2016

Lime Kiln View, Llangrannog

Garn Fawr

Aberaeron, Summer Time

St Martin's Haven

Abereiddy Dog Walk

St David's, Spring

Tenby, Two by Two

A summer evening walk on the harbour at
Tenby inspired this painting. As I made the
initial sketch it became apparent that there
were two people, two dogs, two boats, two
seagulls... This is one of the real pleasures of
being an artist, you train yourself to look very
closely at a scene or object and notice things
that could normally pass you by.

Sea Full of Stars, Laugharne

In 2015 I was invited to hold a solo exhibition at the boathouse in Laugharne as part of the Dylan Thomas centenary celebrations. For this I painted thirteen new paintings of places Dylan Thomas had written about, one of my favourites being Laugharne, where his famous writing shed is and the home he shared with his wife, Caitlin. The original painting envisioned them standing on the bridge over the stream that runs into the Towy, on a soft, summer, moonlit night. As the painting neared completion, the calmness of the scene increased and I began to paint reflections of the stars in the still river, until the Sea became Full of Stars.

Finding Love on the Beach

As often as I'm able I like to walk my dog on the beaches of west Wales, and I usually see other dog walkers, wandering head down, looking at the shells and stones washed up by the tide. This painting imagines a typical Ceredigion beachside village, and two such dog-walkers, one of whom has dropped something precious that the man passing has seen and is astonished by.

And I think – there must be lonely people passing each other on their daily walks, dropping hearts as they pass… and maybe, one day…

Burry Port

People often ask me how long a painting takes to complete. The answer varies. This one took a whole five years from the initial sketch to final details. Paintings always need inspiration; sometimes they'll be 95% complete but lack a little something that I can't quite ascertain. Such was the case with Burry Port, a beautiful, hidden gem of a harbour in Carmarthenshire. It wasn't until I had some visitors at the studio and we were discussing the painting that inspiration occurred – I needed to move the previously very straight and very central path to the lighthouse, making it curved and welcoming. And there it was, done.

Dylan Thomas, Newquay

Summer in Newquay, Ceredigion is a riot of colour and characters. This large (100 x 80cm) painting was undertaken for an exhibition to mark Dylan Thomas' centenary in 2015, and imagines him and Caitlin taking in the view across the harbour of the *"cliff-perched town at the far end of Wales"*.

Dinefwr Spring

"If you take a handful of the soil at Dinefwr and squeeze it in your hand, the juice that will flow from your hands is the essence of Wales."- Wynford Vaughan Thomas.

In 2014 I visited Dinefwr Park, a jewel nestled in the Tiwy Valley, many times over the course of a year to capture the seasons in paint. This lush landscape, *'bright with birds'*, is a joy to be part of. The colours I use in my painting reflect the pleasure I feel being part of this land and the landscape.

Lime Kiln View, Llangrannog

If you're lucky enough, as I am, to walk along Ceredigion's coastal path, you'll come across circular stone structures near to beaches. These are old lime kilns. Limestone blocks were brought in to sandy beaches such as Llangrannog, at high tide, ready for burning in the kilns to turn it into a usable material.

Lime has been used for thousands of years as a mortar, a lime wash for buildings and as a disinfectant in livestock farming. Hydrated lime produces a dry and alkaline environment, which inhibits the growth of bacteria. It's also used to balance the PH of the local soil, which tends to be rather acidic, as the west Wales soils are leached by heavy rainfall. Nice to know.

Garn Fawr, Pembrokeshire

Protected by Strumble Head, this tip of west
Wales, this end of the earth (or so it seems on
a stormy January day), has been painted many
times by three of my most favorite artists in the
last century: John Knapp-Fisher, John Piper
and Graham Sutherland. Each has a different
take on the subject, but each is captivated by
the quality of light here, which is magical and
transforming. Watching as the sun's rays flash
from behind a fast moving cloud, explosion of
light. A sublime, elemental place, I like it best
on an early summer morning, when the abun-
dant wild flowers are still wet with dew and the
light is low. Perfection.

Aberaeron, Summer Time

This is one of my favourite views of one of my favourite places. The harbourside, the Georgian houses, the rowing boats, the summer wild flowers and the old Weigh House – originally used for weighing lime at the harbour. Aberaeron is beautiful all year round, but the busy little harbour comes alive with pleasure boats in the summer, as well as working fishing boats, bunting, and families enjoying the atmosphere. Colour this picture in with the brightest colours you have and see it come to life.

St Martin's Haven

The beach is rarely as quiet as I have painted it, as it's a favourite with divers heading out into the Skomer Marine Nature Reserve, as well as for visitors heading off on regular boats to Skomer Island. The whole area glows with floral colour from heathers, sea poppies and gorse and the air is alive with the calls of thousands of seabirds, including puffins and kittiwakes. The deerless deer park at the very end of the headland is a great place to visit, especially in autumn, when there's a good chance to see seal pups on the beaches below the cliffs.

Abereiddy Dog Walk

My beloved Pembrokeshire is full of little lanes, steep banked in the Welsh style, stone overtopped with soil, from whose hedgerows tumble dog-rose, meadowsweet and honeysuckle, accompanied by outrageous bursts on every corner of bright pink foxgloves. Meander down this lane, its twists and turns revealing glimpses of the light infused sea which no painting could ever do justice to.

But as an artist I have to try. This is the ambiguity that us artists live with daily, constantly desiring to communicate the astounding beauty of a scene, a moment of light, or a flower, whilst knowing that the task is often nearly impossible. After more than twenty-five years of living with this ambiguity I'm still excited by it and am still filled with joy with every painting.

Elliott

St David's, Spring

Britain's smallest city, St David's, guarded by a peninsula of wild and beautiful coast, feels more akin to a cwtchy Welsh village than a grand city, birthplace of a saint and place of pilgrimage. This is a sacred place, hidden in the Valley of Roses, cathedral folded neatly into the green, leafy, raven croaked bowl of close and cottages. This is a place very near to my heart; early family holidays were annually spent here and I return as often as possible during the quieter winter months.

Recently, honoured, inspired and encouraged, I attended the enthronement of a new bishop at the cathedral, Bishop Joanna, the 129th Bishop of St David's, and the first female bishop in Wales. This time, as every time I enter the twelfth century cathedral building, I am awe inspired by its fulfillment of art, mathematics, architecture, craftsmanship, music and philosophy. Hurray for artists, poets, composers and bishops who follow their passions. What a wonderful and diverse world we live in.